Man
of
Covenant
Learning to Walk With God

Russell Gross

urbanpress

Man of Covenant
by Russell Gross
Copyright ©2023 Russell Gross

ISBN 978-1-63360-213-7

For Worldwide Distribution   Printed in the USA

Urban Press
P.O. Box 8881
Pittsburgh, PA 15221-0881
412.646.2780

Dedication

This book is dedicated to all the many men and women who have helped me grow into the man I am and am still becoming. Some were men and women of God, and others were not. Some prayed for me, some taught me, some corrected me, some rebuked me, some pushed me, but all loved and cared enough about me to lead me whether they realized it or not. And God sent all into my life to mold, shape, and help me catch the revelation of not only who God is but also who He called me to be.

So I dedicate this book to my parents, pastors, family, friends, men and women of God, believers and non-believers, co-workers, brothers and sisters in Christ, and others I knew, didn't know or admired, or who somehow influenced me. I say to all, *thank you* from the bottom of my heart!

Introduction

I wrote this book to share what the Lord has shown and taught me about what it means to be a man of covenant over my seventy-plus years on the earth and forty-plus years following Him. Throughout my walk with the Lord, I have been a student of the Word and have worked diligently to apply what I've learned in my everyday life.

During this walk, I have been asked at times to serve in various leadership positions, including men's ministry at both the local church and state prison levels. I've also made most if not all the mistakes that could be made in trying to walk as a man of God. And for some reason which only God knows, He has inspired me at this time and in this season to share what I have learned in hopes that other men's journeys to become who God already sees them to be won't take as long as mine did (and I am still a work in progress).

In this book, I'll be addressing the topic of who a man of covenant really is and what it means to be a man of God from the perspective of a simple formula that I refer to as CIA, which includes 12 key principles of biblical manhood. Neither the CIA formula nor the 12 principles are all there is to know or all it takes to be a man of covenant, but they are what the Lord has revealed to me and what has effectively helped me to move toward being the man God has called me to be. Just so you know, from this point on, I will refer to a man of covenant by its acronym: MoC.

Let's start by considering this quote from the late Dr. Edwin Louis Cole, founder of the Christian Men's Network. I first heard this from Brother Ben Kinchlow on the *700 Club* TV program many years ago: "Being a male is a matter of birth, but being a man is a matter of choice." Just because someone is born a male doesn't automatically mean they are a man, just as biologically bringing a child into the world doesn't automatically make someone a parent.

As with anything in the Kingdom of God, being a man of God or a parent involves a choice—deciding to (or not to) die to one's will and submitting to God's will. In either case, God won't make you choose, you must do so for yourself. And this book will deal with making the choice to live as a man of God instead of a man of the world.

If you are a woman reading this book, please don't tune me out. While it may not apply directly to you, it will help you learn some of the characteristics you should be looking for in the man of God you are seeing now or later. What you learn may also be worthwhile sharing with the men already in your life who you think could benefit from it (husbands, sons, fathers, brothers, uncles, nephews, cousins, etc.).

Therefore, I challenge every one of you reading this book to read it to the end (it's not that long), receive what God has to share concerning biblical manhood, apply it in your life (or if you are a woman, with the men in your life and who will come into your life), and become the MoC God intends you to be. I also want to encourage you to tell others about the book and even share a copy with them so that together we can all grow in biblical manhood.

As you read this book, I want to further encourage you to look up the Scripture references in your own Bible and study them for yourself. Don't just take what I say about the Scriptures as all there is of the truth about a topic. If your study of the

Bible doesn't bear witness to what I say, then you shouldn't accept what I share, or God may have a different revelation to give you than He did me.

So, get ready, stay tuned, and be blessed!

Elder Russell Gross
Mansfield, Massachusetts
March 2023

Section One

The Covenant and the Pillars

This section defines and discusses what "covenant" is all about along with each of the three "pillars" of being a MoC—the fundamental building blocks for living the life of a MoC. Some practical applications of the pillars from my life and the lives of biblical characters are also provided.

Chapter One

COVENANT

Let's begin by defining what a covenant is. It's a binding agreement between two or more parties that can't be broken without penalty, injury, or even death. The concept of covenant has existed since ancient times, and what's called a blood covenant was and is the highest, most holy and solemn of covenants, and *always* involves the shedding blood and *cannot* be broken without paying the price of death (that's obviously why it's called a blood covenant—made in blood and guaranteed in blood). A covenant is serious business, nothing to be played with!

One earthly example of covenant would be the ritual that some gangs practice where new members are cut and mix their blood with other members as a sign of oneness and commitment. But when we talk about a man of covenant in a biblical context, we are talking about a binding agreement between a man and God like the one God established with Abraham through the blood and bodies of sacrificial animals. Now the covenant for born-again believers has been established on the basis of the broken body and shed blood of Jesus.

Every covenant has terms or stipulations that each party agrees they will keep. And when those terms are broken by either party, the one who breaks them must suffer consequences. Penalties are described that may include injury and/or death (in the case of a blood covenant). But praise God! Since He knew men in the flesh could never keep His covenant with Him without breaking it, He's already paid for our (man's) breaking of the covenant through the broken body and shed blood of Jesus, which both established our covenant relationship with God and paid the penalty for our breaking it.

This is not a license to do as we want, thus breaking our covenant with God, for if we do, we'll never be able to walk in the fullness of the blessings and benefits of our covenant with God to the extent God desires us to (this includes eternal life, healing and health, deliverance and restoration, prosperity and peace). Psalm 103:1-5 states,

> "Bless the Lord, O my soul; And all that is within me, bless His holy name! Bless the Lord, O my soul, And forget not all His benefits: Who forgives all your iniquities, Who heals all your diseases, Who redeems your life from destruction, Who crowns you with lovingkindness and tender mercies, Who satisfies your mouth with good things, So that your youth is renewed like the eagle's."

This doesn't indicate that we will be perfect, but we should do all we can to keep our terms of the covenant. But when we do fail, we can repent, receive God's forgiveness and cleansing, and get back on track:

> I beseech you therefore, brethren, by the mercies of God, that you present your bodies a living sacrifice, holy, acceptable to God, which is your reasonable service. And do not be conformed to this world, but be transformed by the

renewing of your mind, that you may prove what is that good and acceptable and perfect will of God (Romans 12:1-2).

If we confess our sins, He is faithful and just to forgive us our sins and to cleanse us from all unrighteousness (1 John 1:9).

Furthermore, if you've given your life to the Lord and are truly in covenant with Him, it's not inherent in your new nature to live a lifestyle of sin. However, when you do stumble and sin, you should experience a sense of conviction in your spirit that you have done something wrong. Then true repentance enters the picture, which involves changing your thinking, so you can thank and speak according to what God says about that area of our life where you have fallen instead of what the world says. Then you can work with Him to bring about permanent change in yourself and your walk with the Lord.

Unlike people, God cannot lie. His Word is truth, and He has sworn by the blood of Jesus (our Covenant-Maker with Him) to keep His Word. And since He can't lie and would have to kill Himself if He didn't keep His Word because of the covenant (a preposterous thought), we can take what He says in His Word and all of the promises therein to the bank, so to speak. They are all better and more valuable and precious than gold!

Therefore, we learn what it means to be a MoC, which includes the terms of our covenant with God (spelled out in His Word). We take it all seriously, get it into our spirit, heart, and mind, careful to live it out in our lives, so we can be the MoC God already sees us being.

Chapter Two

THE THREE PILLARS OF BIBLICAL MANHOOD

These three pillars as I refer to them, or tenets if you will, of biblical manhood provide the foundation for what it means to be a man of covenant and are the basis for the twelve principles of biblical manhood we'll look at later in this book. I also call them the formula or recipe for biblical manhood. Therefore, it's critically important to understand what each pillar means and how to apply them in our lives on a daily basis.

Pillar One: Commitment

The first pillar of the CIA formula begins with "C" and stands for *commitment*. The MoC must be committed. But what does it mean to be committed? It means to be bound or obligated by pledge, promise, or assurance, devoting one's self completely to something. In the case of being a MoC, commitment means being bound (tied to), obligated (required morally and legally), and devoted (zealous, loyal with an ardent attachment by vow) to God and a lifestyle consistent with the

Kingdom of God. More simply stated, commitment as it relates to being the MoC means to be bound or tied to the Word of God, thus living a godly lifestyle.

As we learn from 1 Timothy 1:18-20, being committed involves waging spiritual warfare by faith and with a good conscience:

> This charge I commit to you, son Timothy, according to the prophecies previously made concerning you, that by them you may wage the good warfare, having faith and a good conscience, which some having rejected, concerning the faith have suffered shipwreck, of whom are Hymenaeus and Alexander, whom I delivered to Satan that they may learn not to blaspheme.

In other words, the MoC is dedicated and steadfast, persevering to live a godly lifestyle as a man of God no matter what obstacles and roadblocks one may encounter. It means not giving up in the face of adversity and not being sidetracked or seduced from the ways of God to the ways of the world. Another way to say this is that commitment requires a continual focus on God, His Word, and the Kingdom way of doing things. Second Timothy 2:1-2 states, "You therefore, my son, be strong in the grace that is in Christ Jesus. And the things that you have heard from me among many witnesses, *commit* these to faithful men who will be able to teach others also" (emphasis added).

This passage tells us to be strong in the grace we have through Christ. This means to rely on the power and ability of God to stay the course of living as a godly man rather than a worldly man—rather than relying on your own strength and knowledge, which will eventually fail you. These verses also reveal that commitment not only involves our learning how to stay the course as men of God but also our committing to share what we have learned and applied in our lives with other men so they too can become MoCs—and then teach others to be so as well. A few biblical examples of commitment include:

1. Abraham committing to believe that God could do what He said He would do and make him (Abraham) the father of many nations despite his advanced age and that of his wife Sarah. His commitment was so complete that he was willing to sacrifice his only son Isaac if need be.

2. Moses committing to obey God and lead Israel to the Promised Land, even though he didn't think he was qualified to do so.

3. Our Lord Jesus committing to do God's will rather than His own and die for the sins of all mankind as He knew was God's plan, when His own will would have preferred not to suffer.

A good modern example of a covenant in our own lives would be committing to show up and do the very best we can when we take on a new job or get promoted, while our employer in turn commits to pay us a certain salary or wage. Another would be the vows we make when we get married and the consummation of the marriage on the wedding night, which in God's eyes is a covenant between a man and woman representative of the covenant between God and mankind established through the sacrifice of Jesus on the cross.

Are you committed or ready to be committed to being a MoC, striving to live a godly lifestyle no matter what? I'm not talking being perfect, because none of us is perfect. I'm talking about working to get better each day in your walk with the Lord; learning how to and then living a Kingdom lifestyle; when you do stumble, turning back to God in repentance, receiving forgiveness and cleansing; and living once again in boldness and confidence before God in your walk. However, the choice is always yours, and I pray you will choose to live as a committed man of God and not a man of the world.

Pillar Two: Integrity

The second pillar or ingredient in the formula that makes someone a MoC, the "I," stands for *integrity. Webster's Dictionary* defines integrity *as adherence to moral and ethical principles; honesty; being whole, sound, entire and undiminished.* A life of integrity is a consistent lifestyle based on Kingdom principles and values without compromising those principles and values for anybody or anything. It's being a man of his word, a man who says what he means (based on God's Word) and means what he says, a man who can be counted on to follow through on what he says and commits to do and be.

It's a man who stands for and lives by the Kingdom way of doing things despite what the world system may say is right or what everyone else may be doing. A man of integrity is the MoC, living and walking out the commitment he's made to be bound, tied, and obligated to the Word of God while also striving to live a righteous and godly lifestyle fashioned in the footsteps of Jesus.

Proverbs 10:9 states, "He who walks with

integrity walks securely, but he who perverts his ways will become known." This indicates that if we walk with integrity, doing what is right, we walk securely, but if we don't, our perverse ways will be revealed. We further learn from Titus 2:7 that "in all things showing yourself to be a pattern of good works; in doctrine showing integrity, reverence, incorruptibility." We should show ourselves to be a pattern of good works, displaying integrity, reverence (deep respect and awe), and incorruptibility (morally upright, not debased, not bought or bribed to stray from the ways of God).

A biblical example of integrity would be Job, who continued to trust, stand on, and live by the principles of God, despite what he was going through when tested and tempted by Satan—including his friends who were advising him to give up. Job did question God at times and had some reservations, but he steadfastly stood by what he believed, and God brought him through his "trial by fire" and blessed him more abundantly than he had been blessed before he was tested.

Another good example would be when Daniel defied the Babylonian King by not eating meat or drinking wine the king provided, choosing instead to stick to his vegan-like diet so as not to defile himself by eating the king's unclean food according to Jewish law. God honored Daniel's commitment and gave him great favor with his captors and their king.

One example in my own life of integrity was when I turned down a significant job promotion, which would have involved a home relocation. I put the needs of my immediate family (wife and son) above moving up the "corporate ladder," doing what I believed was "right" as a man of God, husband, and father. Not many years later, God honored my decision by opening the doors for me to move into an even better job without having to relocate.

Being a man of integrity requires dedication, discipline, steadfast effort, and commitment, which is the first pillar. And I would dare say that each and every man, if we are honest with ourselves, can find areas of our lives where we have fallen short or missed the mark as far as integrity is concerned. I know I have.

Therefore, as you read this book, make a decision to work on those areas where you haven't been the man of integrity God expects you to be and already sees you as. It doesn't matter what your past has been like. God hasn't and won't give up on you. You simply must want to change, choose to do so, and then follow through based on what you learn and read in the Word of God.

Pillar Three: Accountability

When I was in grade school and we worked on the alphabet, we used to say A is for apple. But in living as the MoC, the "A" stands for *accountability*. The MoC is accountable, the third pillar of biblical manhood. To be accountable is to take responsibility for one's actions, unlike Adam who tried to put the blame on Eve for letting sin into the human bloodline, who in turn tried to blame the serpent. To be accountable is to stand up and take responsibility for your "world," whether that's your family, workplace, community, or your role in God's Kingdom.

To be accountable is also to stand up and take responsibility to remain submitted to God and the delegated authorities He has placed over you in this earthly realm. This means doing what they command or instruct you to do (unless they ask you to do something illegal, immoral, or ungodly). The source of all authority is God, and His first priority is for His will to be done on earth as in heaven (read Romans 13:1-7 for a description of how you should relate to earthly authority).

Everyone likes to be accountable when being under authority goes well, which is a time to be humble and acknowledge those who actually did the work, glorifying the Lord for His help. But the MoC also needs to be accountable when things or people don't go or do so well. A former pastor of mine used to say that as the man, you are the head of the household as ordained by God, and when something or someone under your authority in the home or with a family member living under your roof goes wrong, you are responsible for dealing with it, whether you caused it or not. That's what real accountability is all about.

Ephesians 5:23 reads, "For the husband is head of the wife, as also Christ is head of the church; and He is the Savior of the body." This shows us the order of accountability in the family. The husband is the head of the wife (and the children as well) just as Christ is the head of the Church, but with headship comes accountability. How can a man as the husband of one wife expect his wife to submit to him or come under his authority if he is not accountable to the other authorities in his own life?

But what does an accountable MoC do when he stumbles, or when something or someone is out of order in the family, home, workplace, church, community, or wherever? He takes responsibility for what took place, deals with the situation according to the Word of God, and, if he has been lax in his duties as the one who is accountable, he repents according to 1 John 1:9 (see above) and

James 5:16: "Confess your trespasses to one an-other, and pray for one another, that you may be healed. The effective, fervent prayer of a righteous man avails much."

The MoC, unlike Adam, doesn't pass the buck, blame someone else, or have an attitude of "I didn't do it so don't blame me." Rather, he steps up, accepts the responsibility, and takes steps to right the situation. This doesn't mean the man of covenant lets those who were involved off the hook. He deals with them as well, correcting them as appropriate. However, he accepts that he is the one who is accountable.

I consider the best biblical description of ac-countability to the command from God to be ac-countable in 2 Corinthians 5:10, which states, "We must all appear before the judgment seat of Christ so that each one may receive what is due for what he has done in the body, whether good or evil." We are *all* going to have to give an account for what we did with everything God made available to us, including His Son Jesus, our wives and kids, our possessions, and those God sent across our paths to help and be helped by. The list could go on and on.

Did I live out God's will and purpose for my life such as write a book, take a missions trip, develop and bless others with my spiritual gifts, serve in my local church, reach lost souls, and make disciples out of people? I would like to think I did, but God will be the judge. Ultimately, doing the very best we can at these things or whatever it is God has called each of us to do is a big part of being accountable. I know I'm not perfect (just ask my wife), but I also know that I want to do all I can to be found pleasing to God, including being accountable for what I did during my time here on this planet.

How about you? In what area(s) of your life are you struggling with authority, whether with those whose authority you are under or with those over whom you have authority? We all have a few areas, so ask God and He will point them out to you. Then accept responsibility for the disorder, repent, and get things in order because that's what the MoC does.

Section Two

Principles of Biblical Manhood

Now that we've covered covenant and the three Pillars of being a MoC—commitment, integrity, and accountability (the CIA formula for the MoC)—let's look at some principles that exemplify these pillars by which the MoC should strive to live, showing how to actually apply the Pillars in your everyday life with some biblical and personal examples. This list of principles is not intended to be exhaustive but are the twelve the Lord has revealed to me which I have found to be most helpful in my walk as a MoC. I believe if you apply them to your life, you will be well on your way to being the MoC God desires you to be.

Chapter Three

PRINCIPLE #1

BE A LEARNED DISCIPLE AND STUDENT OF THE WORD

The first principle of biblical manhood is that *the MoC is a learned disciple of the Lord Jesus Christ and a student of the Word*. By disciple, I don't mean just being saved or born again. That's just the starting point. Being a disciple of Christ means catching the revelation of who He is and His way of doing things. Then you model your lifestyle after His, submitting to His will for your life and being obedient to His commandments.

Being a learned disciple also requires that as you are becoming and after you have become a learned disciple, you make learned disciples out of others by sharing and teaching what you have learned about following Christ so they too can become learned disciples. Jesus' last words talk about this in Matthew 28:18-20:

And Jesus came and spoke to them,

saying, "All authority has been given to Me in heaven and on earth. Go therefore and make disciples of all the nations, baptizing them in the name of the Father and of the Son and of the Holy Spirit, teaching them to observe all things that I have commanded you; and lo, I am with you always, even to the end of the age."

As you see, the Word says *"make"* disciples of all people and to teach them to live by everything Jesus has commanded. To do so means you first have to be a learned disciple yourself, which only comes from being a student of the Word of God.

If you are going to be like Jesus, you need to learn how He thought, behaved, and lived, and you only learn those things from the Word, because Jesus is God's Word manifested in the flesh:

In the beginning was the Word, and the Word was with God, and the Word was God. And the Word became flesh and dwelt among us, and we beheld His glory, the glory as of the only begotten of the Father, full of grace and truth. . . . John bore witness of Him and cried out, saying, "This was He of whom I said, 'He who comes after me is preferred before me, for He was before me'" (John 1:1, 14-15).

Therefore, everything Jesus said and did was God's Word. That's why if we are going to learn and live by the ways of Jesus as learned disciples, we can't just read but have to study the Word and catch the revelation of who Jesus is and how He lived.

The Word of God confirms this very thing. Joshua 1:8 says "This Book of the Law shall not depart from your mouth, but you shall meditate on it day and night, so that you may be careful to do according to all that is written in it; for then you will make your way prosperous, and then you will achieve success." Second Timothy 2:15 states, "Be diligent to present yourself approved to God as a worker who does not need to be ashamed, accurately handling the word of truth." And 2 Timothy 3:16-17 reads, "All Scripture is inspired by God and beneficial for teaching, for rebuke, for correction, for training in righteousness; so that the man *or woman* of God may be fully capable, equipped for every good work."

Studying the Word takes time, effort, and discipline. It's not just reading the Bible, but if you want to capture the insight into what God is truly saying to you so you can apply that in your life, you must invest study time—reading, classes, and other resources. All this involves

- reading, meditating on, praying over, and asking God to open up the Word for you; looking at different versions or translations of the Bible;

- finding the definition of certain words from the Greek and Hebrew as well as English;

- checking with a concordance or other Word study resource;

- talking with other men and women of God who have already caught the revelation of a particular topic or passage you are studying;

- and finally, even using tools like

Google to research answers to some things.

Studying the Word of God should be something you do on a consistent and regular basis, preferably daily. And it's more about the quality of your study at any given time than the quantity of what you study. Knowing a lot of Scripture but not having caught the revelation of what it means or how to apply it in your life doesn't really do you much good. Better to study one chapter or even just a few verses until you "get it"—catch the revelation of what it means and how to apply it in your life.

You also have to understand that this is a lifelong process of continual learning through studying the Word so you can evolve into a learned disciple. You never quite get to where you would want to be. However, as you begin to catch the revelation of Jesus in certain areas of your life, and as you continue to study to go even deeper in that area and learn the ways of Jesus in other areas of life, you can then start making learned disciples by sharing what you have learned. And as you learn even more about being a learned disciple yourself, you can share that with others.

By way of example, let's look at healing. Now there are a lot of references about healing, and most Christians can rattle them off in a minute and "quote" them quite handily when praying for their own or somebody else's healing. But how many of us really have taken the time to study any healing passages to catch the revelation behind them? Perhaps that's why many prayers for healing don't seem to get answered or it takes a very long time for the healing to manifest. We don't take the time or put in the effort to study healing scriptures so we can capture the revelation behind them and "declare" or "confess" that revelation when we want and pray for healing—whether for ourselves or another.

Look at 1 Peter 2:24, which many of us "quote" and stand on when praying for healing. It reads, "And He himself brought our sins in His body on the cross, so that we might die to sin and live for righteousness, by His wounds (stripes) you were healed." We quote the "by His stripes you were healed," but do we really understand the revelation behind those words which is really what unleashes the healing power of Jesus on our behalf?

One revelation you can get when you study this verse (and there are several others) is that because Jesus took all sickness and disease upon himself on our behalf and paid for the root cause of them, which is sin, we believers don't have to bear any sickness and disease in our body. They no longer have any power over us and are illegal intrusions and invaders into our body, attaching themselves to us. Thus through the power in the name of Jesus that has been delegated to us, we have the right to and can "demand" all sickness and disease to leave us and not come back!

In fact, when I pray for healing for myself or someone else, this is how I pray. I no longer just quote Scripture and pray like I'm "begging" God to heal me or someone else, but rather I "declare and confess" the revelation behind verses like 1 Peter 2:24 and command the sickness and disease to leave my body or the body of another so we can walk in the healing and wholeness that is already ours because we are God's sons and daughters through Jesus Christ. I find the manifestation of the answers when I pray this way with revelation from being a student of the Word to be better, quicker, and have longer lasting effects.

So, MoC, are you a learned disciple and student of the Word? Or maybe you have been, but now do not study as much as you should or once did? Whatever the case, get into or back to the discipline of studying the Word of God to become a learned disciple and then start making learned disciples of others.

Chapter Four

PRINCIPLE #2

THE WORD OF GOD IS THE FINAL AUTHORITY AND ABSOLUTE RULE OF CONDUCT FOR OUR LIVES

Principle #2 is something my pastor has taught about many times over the years, and that is that *the Word of God should be the final authority and absolute rule of conduct for the MoC* (and for every believer) *by which they live their lives.* But what does this really mean? For the answer, consider what Jesus said as recorded in Luke 4:4: "But Jesus answered him, saying, 'It is written,

'Man shall not live by bread alone, but by every word of God.'" This indicates that we are to live by *every* word of God. Now to me, *every* word of God means *all* the words of God, not just the ones we like or that are easy to live by or understand.

Hebrews 4:12 states, "For the word of God is living and powerful, and sharper than any two-edged sword, piercing even to the division of soul and spirit, and of joints and marrow, and is a discerner of the thoughts and intents of the heart." This tells us that the Word of God is living, powerful, and can perceive, understand, and know the thoughts and intents of our heart.

Wow! I don't know about you, but I willingly cede, bow down, and come under something as the authority in my life when that something knows everything in my heart, to guide me in all I do and to order my steps. In the power of the Spirit, a book that was written thousands of years ago can detect and help me identify what is going on in my life right now. That's impressive.

The bottom line for the MoC is that if God said it in His Word, then that's it—that's all he needs to hear. Now that doesn't mean you don't have to study for sometimes what appears to be clear in the Bible is part of a truth and must be studied alongside the other things said about that said truth. However, the bottom line is that the MoC accepts that the Word of God presents the standard for how he lives and conducts his life.

If you truly believe that God is God, that He never lies and that His Word is truth, then His Word (His will) should always overrule your will when the two do not agree: "For if our heart condemns us, God is *greater* than our heart, and knows all things" (1 John 3:20, emphasis added). There can be no exceptions! We don't have the option to pick and choose those parts of God's Word that appeal to us. We can't favor those parts we like, or that seem easy to live by, or that won't cause us to abandon what we want to do. When you refer back to Luke 4:4 (see above), it says we should live by *every* word of God, not just some, the ones we like, and so on.

The MoC submits to and willingly comes under the authority of God which comes directly from God or indirectly through the delegated leaders God has placed him under here in the earthly realm, realizing and respecting the source of all authority is God: "Let every soul be subject to the governing authorities. For there is no authority except from God, and the authorities that exist are appointed by God" (Romans 13:1). That means we must die to our own will and live for God's will. It also tells us that every authority God appointed is supposed to be acting or speaking on God's behalf.

Not all do, and we don't always like the delegated authorities we are under. Regardless, we should respect the source of the authority of those delegated authorities who are operating in our lives, and unless they ask us to do anything contrary to God's Word or something illegal, immoral, or ungodly, we should submit and be obedient to what they tell us to do. That's what God's Word being the final authority and absolute rule of conduct for the MoC (and any believer for that matter) looks like!

One example from my own life of how I applied this truth goes back over 50 years when I was fresh out of college and in my first job. I was working as a telecommunications construction manager as part of a program in which college graduates were placed in a managerial position and given one year to demonstrate that they had middle- to upper-management potential. If they did, they were given a permanent position and "fast-tracked" to move up the corporate ladder. If they didn't, they were summarily dismissed at the end of the one year. In general, only about 30% succeeded.

In the assignment, a common practice at the end of each month was to have all the jobs that had begun in the previous three months reviewed by somone in the accounting department in the construction manager's office. This helped ensure that credit was being taken for as many construction operations within each job as possible to accumulate as many "completions" as possible, which was one measure of monthly district evaluation. The construction manager and their district manager had to sign off on each completion.

After a few months had gone by and I had "learned the ropes" of how things were done, it became apparent to me that credit was being taken for work operations not actually completed through what were obviously incorrect interpretations of the completion rules, something that had always been done. So I decided not to sign off on work operations that were not actually completed or didn't qualify as being credited as per the rules. This made my area's and my manager's district work order productivity start to fall.

When my district manager called me on the carpet about this, I told him that I could not lie about it because it was neither right nor legal because it was dishonest and actually sinful. Now I wasn't saved at this point in my life, but I'd had enough of both a good upbringing by my parents and teaching on God's Word from attending church with my grandmother that I knew God didn't approve of or honor lying of any kind.

Although I was fearful this might cost me my job, after the year was up I was deemed to have potential enough to be given a permanent position, which I attribute in large part to choosing to make the Word of God the final authority and absolute rule of conduct for my life.

Joshua was such a man who made the Word of God the final authority and absolute rule of conduct for his life, and before his death he exhorted all the people of Israel in Joshua Chapter 24 to follow God and Him only. Note in particular what he said in verses 14-15, especially the last words of verse 15 :

> "Now, therefore, fear the Lord and serve Him in sincerity and truth; and do away with the gods which your fathers served beyond the Euphrates River and in Egypt, and serve the Lord. But if it is disagreeable in your sight to serve the Lord, choose for yourselves today whom you will serve: whether the gods which your fathers served, which were beyond the Euphrates River, or the gods of the Amorites in whose land you are living; *but as for me and my house, we will serve the Lord*" (emphasis added).

Twice in verse 15, including the last 12 words, these verses point out that each and every one of us has to make an intentional and purposeful choice to follow God, which we do by living according to the directives in His Word, which can only do if we've studied the Word, as we discussed in the last chapter, and then apply it in our lives.

Jesus is the perfect biblical example of making the Word of God the final authority and absolute rule of conduct for our lives. When in the Garden of Gethsemane before He was taken captive and began the final journey of His purpose to die for the sins of all mankind, He yielded His will to that of the Father. In Matthew 26:39 and 42 He says,

> "My Father, if it is possible, let this cup pass from Me; yet not as I will, but as You will." . . . He went away again a second time and prayed, saying, "My Father, if this cup cannot pass away unless I drink from it, Your will be done."

And in Mark 14:36, Jesus said, "Abba! Father! All things are possible for You; remove this cup from Me; yet not what I will, but what You will."

So, MoC, do you strive to make the Word of God the final authority and absolute rule of conduct in your life? The decision to do so is between you and God, but the good news is that if the answer is no, it's not too late. Be honest with yourself and God (who already knows), repent, commit before God to make His Word the final authority and absolute rule of conduct for how to live your life, and ask God to help you (and He will).

Chapter Five

PRINCIPLE #3

LIVE RIGHTEOUSLY

Principle #3 of being a MoC is that *the MoC strives to live righteously* (a godly lifestyle modeled after Jesus), *not deliberately or intentionally disobeying the Word of God* (which is commonly referred to as sinning). I am not talking about being perfect, because as long we live in this sinful flesh, we can never be perfect. That's why God made provision for us when we do stumble, fall, or sin in 1 John 1:9, as discussed earlier. What I am saying is that we should do all we can to live righteously according to the Word of God. That should be our nature as children of God through Christ, rather than the worldly nature we were born with, which accepts whatever the world or our selfish desires prescribe as correct.

Webster defines righteousness as *the quality or state of being just or rightful, and righteous as being morally right or justifiable*. Furthermore, one definition of being just is *to be guided by truth, reason, justice, and fairness*. Righteousness therefore is a position or place one is in, which is determined by their behavior. It is being in good stead or right standing with something or somebody.

As it relates to being a MoC, righteousness means being in right standing with God, which is possible only because of Jesus' redemptive work completed on our behalf. Through His sacrifice, He imparted to us His righteousness when we are in Him, which has nothing to do with anything we did or could ever do. However, it's up to us to live out that righteousness in our everyday lives as men, and since Jesus is our role model for living a godly lifestyle that is pleasing to God and conforms to His will for our lives, we should look to His lifestyle as to how we are to strive to live righteously.

In Titus 2:11-12, Paul wrote, "For the grace of God that brings salvation has appeared to all men, teaching us that, denying ungodliness and worldly lusts, we should live soberly, righteously, and godly in the present age." We are told we should not live as the world does, pursuing that which is ungodly and lusting after things that gratify our flesh. Rather, we are to live soberly. This is self-control or reining in our passion and lust for things of the flesh through discipline and righteous living (conforming to God's will for our lives), and godly attitudes (thinking that which is pleasing to God). In other words, don't sin! We learn in 1 John 5:17a that "all unrighteousness is sin." Sin is anything outside the will of God or contrary to God's Word. Another way to define it is missing the mark— falling short of the requirements spelled out in the Word of God.

What's more, this is all for your own good; God knows how to have you live so you can enjoy happiness and fulfillment. Paul wrote in 1 Corinthians 10:21, "You cannot drink the cup of the

Lord and the cup of demons; you cannot partake of the table of the Lord and the table of demons." James wrote in James 4:1-4,

> What is the source of quarrels and conflicts among you? Is the source not your pleasures that wage war in your body's parts? You lust and do not have, so you commit murder. And you are envious and cannot obtain, so you fight and quarrel. You do not have because you do not ask. You ask and do not receive, because you ask with the wrong motives, so that you may spend what you request on your pleasures. You adulteresses, do you not know that friendship with the world is hostility toward God? Therefore whoever wants to be a friend of the world makes himself an enemy of God.

Both these passages clearly explain that you can't live with one foot in the world and one foot in the Kingdom of God and expect to be pleasing to God. That's not living righteously! In fact, as James points out, living that way, not always putting "the God way" above the desires of the flesh, makes you an enemy of God! It's like committing adultery and cheating on God. And God is not going to stand for or honor that way of living.

God spoke of three good examples of biblical MoCs who lived righteously through the prophet Ezekiel in Ezekiel 14:12-14,

> Then the word of the LORD came to me, saying, "Son of man, if a country sins against Me by being unfaithful, and I stretch out My hand against it, destroy its supply of bread, send famine against

it, and eliminate from it both human and animal life, even though these three men, Noah, Daniel, and Job were in its midst, by their own righteousness they could only save themselves," declares the Lord GOD."

I highly recommend you study what the Bible has to say about these men on your own, and when you do, you'll discover God said of Noah in Genesis 6:9 that "Noah was just a man and perfect in his generations and walked with God." Of Job God said in Job 1:8 and 2:3 "There is none like him in the earth, a perfect and upright man . . . one who feareth God, escheweth evil." Of Daniel, God said as recorded in Daniel 9:23 and 10:11 and 17 that he was greatly loved by God and thus an angel was sent to answer his prayers. These were all men just like you and me. They weren't perfect, but each one had a heart for God and made it their priority to live righteously. When they fell, they turned back to God, repented, and resumed striving to live righteously. God honored that in their lives.

So how do you choose to strive to live? As a MoC living by the Word of God, or as a man of the flesh following the ways of the world? Or are you sometimes wishy-washy, occasionally choosing to follow God while at other times choosing to follow the world, which is a lifestyle that's no better than not following God at all. God is a jealous God and wants all of you, not just the parts in which you are willing to yield your will to His.

Whatever your answer may be as to how you will live or the level of commitment to God you will manifest, you have a choice to make as to how to live your life from this day forward. I pray you choose to strive to be a MoC, living righteously and obediently to God's Word, and not sinfully—deliberately and intentionally choosing the ways of the world instead of the ways of God.

Chapter Six

PRINCIPLE #4
REPENTENCE

The fourth principle of being a MoC is that *when the MoC sins, he repents*. By repentance, I don't mean just admitting to God that you've sinned, saying you are sorry, and receiving His forgiveness and cleansing according to 1 John 1:9. That is certainly a part of repentance, but true repentance means to change the way you think so that it produces lasting behavioral change in an area where you have sinned repeatedly.

Romans 12:2 tells us, "And do not be conformed to this world, but be transformed by the renewing of your mind, that you may prove what is the good and acceptable and perfect will of God." We should not do or live according to what the world says is acceptable, because the world is still under the dominion of Satan whose only purpose is to deceive and destroy us and divert us from God's will for our lives.

Instead, we need to be transformed or changed by the renewing of our minds, which is to change the way we think, abandoning our worldly mindset and adopting a godly one. This is what true repentance is all about, and how one brings about lasting behavioral change instead of short-term changes that come from only confessing our sins and asking for forgiveness, while eventually going back to the worldly ways of our thinking.

True repentance is a process, not an event that takes place in a moment of time. Repentance takes time, work, and effort on your part if it is to have lasting results. Repentance is about replacing the garbage in your heart, soul, and mind that led to your sin in the first place with what the Word of God says concerning that area of your life where you are not meeting God's standard. It not only takes time and effort, but discipline as well, since you have to study and meditate on the Word of God related to the area of your life where you sinned until you have firmly established an understanding of what God says on the matter, replacing what you have learned of the world's ways with those of God.

Then, once your spirit and soul have lined up with the Word of God, you can start applying what God says about that area of your life where you have sinned, and in time your body, mind, and actions will line up with the Word as well. Let me repeat, and I can't emphasize this enough: Repentance is a process, not an event. It doesn't happen overnight or simply by confessing or agreeing once or twice with what God says about an area of your life. Rather, it involves you repeating over time what God says about your optimal situation as compared to the present situation, and in time your behavior and walk will align with what God says as found in His Word.

There are so many examples of repentance throughout the Bible, but I want to give you three references you can dig deeper into on your own. Let's start with God Himself in Genesis 6 (emphasis on verses 5 through 8). After He saw how evil mankind had become, He was sorry and repentant about having created mankind and declared His desire to wipe it out along with everything else that was living. However, Noah found favor with God, and we know through Noah God restored mankind.

In Psalms 32 and 51 we see the story of Bathsheba and David and how David was repentant after his transgression with Bathsheba against her husband Uriah. And in Luke 15:11-32, we have the story of the prodigal son. Once he "came to his senses," got into his right mind, changed his thinking, and realized who he was and who his father was, he determined to repent and go back to his father, ask for forgiveness, and change his ways. Now there's a lot more to this story than just repentance, but I believe it is a good example of what repentance involves.

One example in my own life is in an area that most men deal with for the better part of their lives, which is lust, or more specifically sexual lust or sexual immorality. And while this takes many forms depending upon the individual, most if not all men fall prey to it at some point in their lives. Whatever form it takes, it requires true repentance to walk in the deliverance and freedom that Jesus paid the price for us to have.

In my own case, once I caught the revelation of repentance and studied the Word, I found that the Bible has a lot to say about sexual immorality. However, the passage I stood and still stand on most often is found in the first three words in 1 Corinthians 6:18-20: "Flee sexual immorality." That, along with verse 3 from 1 Thessalonians 4:3-8, made a big difference in my approach to sexual purity: "For this is the will of God, your sanctification; that is, that you abstain from sexual immorality."

Now when I studied these passages, I caught the revelation that sexual immorality is from the devil; that Jesus took all forms of sexual immorality on Himself on my behalf; that sexual immorality has no power over me unless I choose to let it; and that I have the delegated power (authority and ability) from Jesus to bind sexual immorality and command it to leave me and never come back in His name! When I started to confess these Scriptures and walked in the revelation behind them over my life, in time I began to walk in freedom and victory over sexual immorality. Glory be to God!

I also came into the revelation that as a man, the devil will attack me with thoughts of lust and sexual immorality for the rest of my life, so I can't ever let my guard down. As such, I make repenting of sexual immorality a part of my lifestyle and confess the Scriptures above and the revelation behind them over my life on a regular basis, especially when the devil tries to tempt me with sexual immorality. Am I perfect? No! But since I have made repentance from sexual immorality as well as other lusts of the flesh a part of my lifestyle, I stumble much less than I used to, and when I do, it's usually by letting thoughts of sexual immorality linger in my mind longer than I should (which is still sin), which if I'm not careful will lead to living them out in my life.

We repent one area of our life at a time as the Spirit leads us. If we try to change every area that is off at the same time, we won't be successful because that will be too much change for any of us to absorb and retain at one time. So ask God where to start, to show you an area of your life He wants you to address first. When you do, I can almost guarantee that what He wants to deal with first is not the area you want to deal with first—or even talk with Him about. But if God puts His finger on an area, that's where you need to start.

So, MoC, man up when you stumble, not only to receive God's forgiveness and cleansing, but also to renew your mind and be transformed—something all of us need to do on a daily basis.

Chapter Seven

PRINCIPLE #5

PLACING THE NEEDS OF FAMILY AND OTHERS ABOVE HIS OWN

Principle 5 of being a MoC is that *the MoC places the needs of his family and others above his own.* The CIA formula of manhood is really an expression of God's love which He has placed in every believer as described in 1 Corinthians 13:4-7:

> Love suffers long and is kind; love does not envy; love does not parade itself, is not puffed up; does not behave rudely, *does not seek its own,* is not provoked, thinks no evil; does not rejoice in iniquity, but rejoices in the truth; bears all things, believes all things, hopes all things, endures all things (emphasis added).

Note the emphasis I put on five words in

verse five: "does not seek its own." This phrase means that you put the well-being and best interests of others above your own. You do that by giving of yourself to the fullest for the benefit of others without expecting anything in return. That is the God-kind of love—agape love.

The covenant of marriage is a good example of putting the well-being and best interests of another above your own. It's a model of how the Church is to function on the earth, as described in Ephesians 5:25: "Husbands, love your wives, just as Christ also loved the church and gave Himself for her." This teaches men that as husbands we should love our wives just as Christ loved the church and "gave Himself for her," which is the part I really want you to see as a MoC. We as men need to grasp this revelation in those four words. We need to stop being selfish and childish and grow up so we can become who God called us to be.

We as men sometimes prefer to emphasize what is taught in the previous verses, Ephesians 5:22-24:

> Wives, submit to your own husbands, as to the Lord. For the husband is head of the wife, as also Christ is head of the church; and He is the Savior of the body. Therefore, just as the church is subject to Christ, so let the wives be to their own husbands in everything.

When we do that, we miss the point of verse 25 which is that if we expect our wives to submit to us, we need to lead and love them as Jesus does the church—not lording it over them but leading them and treating them like the gift from God they are.

We can find another example of putting the best interests and needs of others above our own when we read Ephesians 6:4, which discusses the family from God's point of view: "And you, fathers, do not provoke your children to wrath, but bring them up in the training and admonition of the Lord." Fathers shouldn't provoke our children by "going off on them," but rather raise them to know, follow, and love the ways of the Lord.

Of course, you discipline your children when necessary, but you do so in love and speak positive things into their lives that will encourage them to pursue their purpose and be all they can be. That is much more effective than just telling them they can't be this or do that. You can't take it out on them because you didn't get the type of love and encouragement you craved when you were growing up. Jesus said in Mark 12:28-31,

> Then one of the scribes came, and having heard them reasoning together, perceiving that He had answered them well, asked Him, "Which is the first commandment of all?" Jesus answered him, "The first of all the commandments is: 'Hear, O Israel, the Lord our God, the Lord is one. And you shall love the Lord your God with all your heart, with all your soul, with all your mind, and with all your strength.' This is the first commandment. And the second, like it, is this: 'You shall love your neighbor as yourself.' There is no other commandment greater than these."

Jesus reminded us that the two greatest commandments are to love God with all our being and to love our neighbors (other people, *all* other people) as we love ourselves—putting the needs of others above our own.

Do you put the needs of your family and others above your own as an expression of God's love for and in you? Are there times when you act selfishly and put yourself first when you should have or could have put the needs of your family or others first? If we're honest, most of us would have to respond "sometimes" to both of these questions.

Now there are times when you need to put yourself first, such as in your personal relationship with God and in obedience to a word or instruction from God (which many times is actually for the benefit of someone other than you). But if we are obedient to Matthew 6:33, "But seek first the kingdom of God and His righteousness, and all these things shall be added to you" as we seek God's Kingdom first, we should for the most part as MoCs find ourselves putting the needs of our family and others ahead of our own.

The book of Nehemiah is a great biblical example of a man of God putting the needs of others above his own. When you read his story on your own, you will see how much he went through to restore Jerusalem for the sake of his people. Nehemiah was a Jew and high official, specifically a butler or cupbearer, in the Persian court to the King in Susa during the time when the people of Judah were taken captive in Babylon. He had it in his heart to rebuild the city of his people who were living in exile and great distress. The wall around Jerusalem was broken down and the city was in ruins.

Nehemiah's compassion for his people moved him to intercede before God for them, despite their sinful ways, asking God to give him favor with the King to get permission to rebuild the walls around Jerusalem. God honored Nehemiah's sacrifice of his own self-interests for the sake of his people and homeland by giving him favor with the king who appointed Nehemiah as governor of

Judah, even giving him the supplies he needed to rebuild the wall.

While there are a number of lessons that can be learned from this account, the lesson I want to point out is that Nehemiah could have stayed where he was, in the king's court, with a high position and "comfortable" lifestyle. But he didn't forget who he was, where he came from, or who his people were. Rather, he "got out of his comfort zone" by putting the needs of his people above his own and led the efforts to rebuild the wall around Jerusalem and restore the capital or major city of his homeland.

Earlier I shared about a time in my own life midway through my corporate career when I had a chance for a major promotion that would have propelled me up "the corporate ladder" but it would have required a major relocation several states away from where my family and I were living. Instead of accepting the promotion and moving ahead in my career, I put the needs of my wife and son above my own, realizing that at that time in their lives, it was best to stay in the area where we were—also remembering the sacrifices my wife and son had already made through earlier relocations of our home to help further my career.

But just as God honored Nehemiah when he put the needs of his people above his own needs, God did the same for me. While turning down that promotion hurt my career advancement in the short term, in the long term God opened doors for me that I had never imagined possible, and I was able to advance my career much further than if I had taken that earlier promotion.

So men, the lesson is simple but clear: Stop being selfish and step up and be who God called you to be by putting the needs of your family and others above your own.

Chapter Eight

PRINCIPLE #6

HONOR, RESPECT, LOVE, AND RAISE UP

Principle #6 of being a MoC has a three-fold-family focus and that is *the MoC honors and respects his parents, loves his wife like Jesus loves the church, and raises his children according to the word of God.* Yes, some of this is a carry-over from Principle #5 but it is worth examining further. The biblical basis for this principle can be found throughout Ephesians 5 and 6.

"Children, obey your parents in the Lord, for this is right. 'Honor your father and mother,' which is the first commandment with promise: 'that it may be well with you and you may live long on the earth'" (Ephesians 6:1-3). This passage tells us it is right for children to obey and honor our parents with the promise that if we do, it will go well with us and we will have a long life on the earth. That's quite powerful. I wonder why all people then do not just honor and respect their parents?

Some would say they never knew their father or mother, others would say their father or mother walked out on the family when they were young, while still others may say their father or mother, while present, wasn't a good parent. These are all painful experiences, but none are valid excuses for not honoring and respecting the earthly vessels God used to bring you into the world. You only have one biological mother and father, so honor them no matter what. God honored them by blessing them with you, so you should honor them as well.

The same holds true for step-parents and others who may have raised you or had a hand in raising you in the absence of biological parents. Being a parent is not just about bringing a child into the world biologically but also and more importantly about raising a child up to know how they should live.

Even if you can only pray for your parents from afar or pray for them if they have passed from this world, do so, and honor them. Reflect on how they raised you to understand some things to do and not to do with your own children, but still honor them. Why? Because God commands you to, and earlier we learned that the Word of God should be the final authority and absolute rule of conduct for your life.

Therefore, as MoCs, let us submit to God's will by honoring and respecting our parents whenever and however we can. We do this not just because God says to, but also to express our love and gratitude for the love our parents gave and the sacrifices they made for us, even though we may not have realized what they were doing at the time.

I know in my own life that although I had

differences of opinion and at times was upset with my parents, once I caught this revelation, I honored them as best I could by submitting to them when I was growing up—even if I didn't always agree or want to do what they were asking or telling me to do. I celebrated them on their birthdays and wedding anniversary. I called home when I was out on my own at last once a week to talk with them, just to tell them I loved them. I sought their counsel and advice on issues of life I was encountering as a young adult, such as whether or I not I should marry the woman I finally did take as my wife. Finally, I cared for them when each became ill late in their lives.

And as I honored them in these ways, and still honor their memory even though they are no longer here, I came to realize what a blessing to me they were and how blessed I was to have them in my life until my late sixties when each of them passed just short of 95 years of age. And I will always remember what each of them said to me in their own way just before they transitioned: "I'm so proud of you. You were a good son, and I love you so very much."

In Luke 2:51 is the account when Joseph and Mary took Jesus with them when he was 12 years old to Jerusalem for the Feast of the Passover. After they departed for home, they realized He was not with them and had to return to Jerusalem and search for days to find Him. They finally found Him in the Temple where He told them He had to be in His Father's house. The gospel writer recorded that after that, He went back to Nazareth with them and continued to be subject to them. So if Jesus honored His earthy parents by coming under their authority, shouldn't we?

The second part of principle #6 of the CIA of

being a MoC is that he loves his wife as Christ loves the church. Let's go back and look at Ephesians 5 once again, this time looking at the entire passage:

> Husbands, love your wives, just as Christ also loved the church and gave Himself for her, that He might sanctify and cleanse her with the washing of water by the word, that He might present her to Himself a glorious church, not having spot or wrinkle or any such thing, but that she should be holy and without blemish. So husbands ought to love their own wives as their own bodies; he who loves his wife loves himself. For no one ever hated his own flesh, but nourishes and cherishes it, just as the Lord does the church. For we are members of His body, of His flesh and of His bones. "For this reason a man shall leave his father and mother and be joined to his wife, and the two shall become one flesh." This is a great mystery, but I speak concerning Christ and the church. Nevertheless let each one of you in particular so love his own wife as himself, and let the wife see that she respects her husband (Ephesians 5:25-33).

Let's examine this passage. These verses tell us how Christ loved the Church, and since the covenant of marriage is a mirror image of the relationship of Christ to the Church, MoCs should love their wives likewise—building her up, treating her as their queen, encouraging her, supporting her, helping her to become spotless and without blemish, treating her like the gift from God she is, loving her as they love themselves.

At the same time, this passage also tells us we should instruct and lead our wives in the things of God including leading them in prayer and praying with them daily, because husbands and wives who pray together stay together. And when we learn to lead our wives by serving and supporting them in this way, they will want to submit to us, just as the Church does to Christ.

Men, we need to trade in the "king of the castle" attitude of worldly husbands for the "servant-leader" attitude Christ has for the Church. When we do, we can experience the depth of spiritual intimacy God desires for us to have with our wives, which leads to greater intimacy in all other areas of marriage. Love your wife as Christ does the Church.

My current wife and I were married three years ago as I write when I was two weeks short of 71 and she was 72. Before we got married, we took the time to talk about a lot of those things that were going to impact our marriage. We talked about where we would live, how we would share the household chores, who would handle the finances, our families, our likes and dislikes, where we would go to church, and how we would serve in that church.

We talked about our faith, and things in our lives that normally we don't like to talk about so we both really knew about each other. We talked about communication, sex, and money, the three issues that tend to impact every single relationship. We also talked about the five languages of love using Gary Chapman's book as a reference (words of affirmation, acts of service, receiving gifts, quality time, and physical touch) because it's important to understand how your spouse prefers to be communicated with, and what his or her one or two primary love languages are. We also try to keep the spice in our marriage now that we are married by having a "date night" every Friday night, for which I always get my wife roses each week.

Now this doesn't mean either of us or our marriage is perfect, but we make it a point not to let our heads go to sleep on our pillows at night with anything between us. Since before we were married we talked about how to communicate effectively with each other, we're usually able to work things through, not always in one day or one night as sometimes it takes several days—but we are usually able to work things out.

Now my role as husband in the marriage is to lead my wife because as a husband I am over her as Christ is over the Church. But Christ doesn't lead the Church by "lording" it over the Church. He leads the church by serving the church and that's how I try to lead my wife. I try to build her up, edify her, treat her as the gift she is to me from God, and lead her in spiritual things. This doesn't mean that my voice is the only voice being heard. I listen to my wife and because we can communicate with each other, we're able to work through things and reach a decision on how to move forward. Then it's my job to lead us as we walk out the decision we agreed upon. As a result, my wife respects me and can submit to me as her husband.

One last thing I am learning to do is to treat my wife as the gift from God that she is by saying "I'm sorry" and "Please forgive me" when I'm wrong. It's also so very important in a marriage to remember that there are three people involved in the marriage: the husband, the wife, and Jesus. We need to listen to and consult with Jesus just as much if not more so than with our spouse.

The third part of principle #6 of the CIA of

being a man of covenant is that the MoC raises his children according to the Word of God. Ephesians 6:4 says, "And you, fathers, do not provoke your children to wrath, but bring them up in the training and admonition of the Lord." As fathers, we shouldn't provoke (push or drive) our children to wrath (rage or rebellion), but rather bring them up in the training and admonition of the Lord. What does this really mean? What it doesn't mean is that we should refrain from disciplining our children, allowing them to do whatever they want to do.

What it does mean is that we should raise our children based on the Word of God, help them develop godly and righteous habits in areas such as prayer, giving, honor and respect, good behavior, regular church attendance, etc. And, we should do this out of and with love, supporting and encouraging them, letting them know there isn't anything they can't achieve, confessing the blessings and promises of God over their lives.

When we do have to discipline them, we do so appropriately and out of love, so they understand why they are being disciplined, explaining right from wrong (even if they don't understand it at first). We do this rather than coming down hard on them all the time, putting them down, or never seeming to have a good word or words of encouragement for them (provoking them to wrath). So, MoC, raise and train your children in the admonition (reprimand, scolding, advice, and counsel) of the Lord (not of the world).

As I think back on being a father and raising my son, there are times I wish I could go back and do it all over again knowing what I know now. But obviously I can't. However, when I stop to think and look at my son and see the man he has grown up to be, I realize that I didn't do such a bad job after all. I've also come to realize that it's never too late. I really cherish and treasure those moments when my son comes to me as an adult and asks me for advice, and I have the opportunity to continue to speak into his life. If it's not too late for me, it's not too late for you to still be the parent your children need you to be to guide them in the way they should go.

This is also true for me with my stepson. Unfortunately for him, his natural father wasn't around very much when he was growing up, and I really appreciate all the one-on-one discussions and conversations I have with him when he asks me for advice, guidance, and direction. And as we have these discussions, I realize that I did a lot of this with my own son when he was growing up and still have the opportunity to do so now that he's an adult. That gives me great joy and happiness being able to still speak into their lives to help them in their ongoing growth into the men God has called them to be.

Lastly men, speaking about sons and stepsons, children and step children, I consider both my sons to be my sons (no step), because being a father is not only or primarily about making children, but more importantly about raising and guiding children to become who God created them to be.

As MoCs, we have to ask ourselves: Do we honor and respect our parents, love our wives as Christ loved the church and raise our children in the things of God? Be honest with yourself, and wherever you find yourself not doing any of these things, repent and get that area right in your life as God wants each of us to do.

Chapter Nine

PRINCIPLE #7

WALK BY FAITH, NOT BY SIGHT

Principle #7 of biblical manhood is that *the MoC "walks by faith, not by sight" (2 Corinthians 5:7)*. All too often we say we have faith in God, but then allow our behaviors and attitudes to be dictated by our emotions, feelings, and circumstances instead of the Word of God. Paul wrote in 2 Corinthians 4:18, "While we do not look at the things which are seen, but at the things which are not seen. For the things which are seen are temporary, but the things which are not seen are eternal." Our circumstances we can see with our natural eyes are only for a season or short period of time.

Therefore, we shouldn't allow them or how we feel about them to dictate how we respond to them or how we live our lives—how we think, act, or react. This is because they are temporary and won't last very long. However, we see the things of God through our spiritual eyes which we can only read about but can't see with our natural eyes. That is how we catch the revelation through

God's Word. And these things are eternal and last forever and thus are what we should focus on, allowing them to determine and direct how we live our lives.

In other words, we should live our lives based on the Word of God while not responding to our circumstances or what we see, which is a simple definition of walking by faith and not by sight. Faith is trusting God to do what He said in His Word He would do; or as I like to say in my seminars, faith is the reality of the future good (hope) we're expecting based on God's Word, the proof (evidence) that this future good already exists, and the confidence that we will come to have it.

Faith functions by seeing what God has promised us in His Word with the spiritual eyes of our heart or spirit, receiving and believing what the Word of God says about our situation without any doubt in our hearts. We choose not to accept what we feel or what our emotions or circumstances would seem to say; confess the Word of God over our situation; and then move, act, and live based on our belief of God's Word in our heart and the confession of that Word out of our mouth over our lives.

For example, we saw earlier that the Bible says in the latter part of 1 Peter 2:24 "by His wounds [some versions say stripes] we were healed." So when you study that further, you find that this is saying Jesus took every sickness and disease that could ever come upon us on Himself, paying the price for the root cause of sin on our behalf, so we don't have to carry sin, sickness, or disease in our bodies—unless we let them, which we are capable of doing since we still live in sinful flesh. And when the sickness occurs and tries to overtake us, we have the right as children of God to bind them up by what the Word of God says and command them to leave us in Jesus' name—and they must go!

Now that may be an instantaneous or miraculous healing, but most times it's progressive as we exercise our faith. And how do we do that? First by receiving and believing what the Word of God says, including the revelation behind the Word, as we saw in 1 Peter 2:24. This can take some time to do through meditation, confession, prayer, and talking with other believers who have already caught this revelation and experienced it in their own lives. Once you believe it, then you confess it verbally over and against the sickness or disease trying to attack you. Then you need to act on what you believe and are confessing.

This is exactly what I did when my lungs were severely damaged after I had COVID back in early 2020. I studied the Word to reinforce my understanding and revelation of 1 Peter 2:24 and other Scriptures related to healing. Then I confessed them over my life, declaring I was already healed by what Jesus did for me and commanding the attack on my lungs to leave me in Jesus' name. Then I acted on that belief and confession by trying to breathe more normally each day, with and without the oxygen tube in my nose.

The more I acted on my belief and confession, the stronger my lungs became. Some days I made progress, but on others I didn't. But by continually exercising my faith, over a relatively short period of time (three months to be exact), my lungs were completely restored despite the doctors not knowing why my breathing had not gotten back to normal considering I no longer had COVID. They even wanted to crack my chest open and do a lung biopsy. You see, I didn't deny my lungs were damaged, but my confession and actions were based on my belief in my heart concerning what God said, not what my condition said.

Our circumstances are real and factual, so we should not deny they exist. However, they are not the ultimate truth; the Word of God is the truth. And the truth of God's Word will set you free: "Then Jesus said to those Jews who believed Him, "If you abide in My word, you are My disciples indeed. And you shall know the truth, and the truth shall make you free" (John 8:31-32). Faith will always change the facts and reality of our circumstances, if we are exercising it by receiving, believing, confessing, and acting on the Word of God.

You can also look to the many men and women of God in the Bible as examples of people who lived their lives by faith, such as those referenced in Hebrews 11:4-11:

> By faith Abel offered to God a better sacrifice than Cain, through which he was attested to be righteous, God testifying about his gifts, and through faith, though he is dead, he still speaks. By faith Enoch was taken up so that he would not see death; and he was not found because God took him up; for before he was taken up, he was attested to have been pleasing to God. And without faith it is impossible to please Him, for the one who comes to God must believe that He exists, and that He proves to be One who rewards those who seek Him. By faith Noah, being warned by God about things not yet seen, in reverence prepared an ark for the salvation of his household, by which he condemned

the world, and became an heir of the righteousness which is according to faith. By faith Abraham, when he was called, obeyed by going out to a place which he was to receive for an inheritance; and he left, not knowing where he was going. By faith he lived as a stranger in the land of promise, as in a foreign land, living in tents with Isaac and Jacob, fellow heirs of the same promise; for he was looking for the city which has foundations, whose architect and builder is God. By faith even Sarah herself received ability to conceive, even beyond the proper time of life, since she considered Him faithful who had promised.

So, MoC, how are you walking or living your life? Do you live by faith in the Word of God? Or when the deceitfulness of this life and world system brings circumstances into your life that challenge your faith, do you stand strong in faith on the Word of God or do you give in to the circumstances?

Each of us needs to ask ourselves these questions, honestly answer them, and repent in those areas where we have been walking more by sight than faith. Then we need to strengthen our faith through study and confession of the Word and praise and worship of God. Then we can truly walk by faith and not by sight as the MoCs we are!

If you want to gain a deeper understanding and revelation of biblical faith, you might want to read another book I wrote, *Faith: The Currency of The Kingdom*, available on Amazon and my website (faithprinciples.net).

Chapter Ten

PRINCIPLE #8

HAVE A DEVOTIONAL LIFE AND PRAY DAILY

Principle #8 of biblical manhood is that *the MoC has a devotional life and prays daily*. Jesus had a devotional life and prayed daily, so we should too. And our devotional life among other things should be an expression of our total love of God: "You shall love the LORD your God with all your heart, with all your soul, and with all your strength" (Deuteronomy 6:5), and submission to His authority and commandments in our life:

> "But take careful heed to do the commandment and the law which Moses the servant of the LORD commanded you, to love the LORD your God, to walk in all His ways, to keep His commandments, to hold fast to Him, and to serve Him with all your heart and with all your soul" (Joshua 22:5).

We do this with the realization that all power and authority come from God, as it says in Romans 13:1b: "For there is no authority except from God." We should worship and praise God corporately, pray together with our families and brothers and sisters in Christ, and not forsake assembling with one another. Those are all directives from the Bible, but they don't constitute a devotional life.

Having a devotional life means being in the presence of God one on one; it's your private time with God. It's a time to pray, have a two-way dialogue with your heavenly Father, during which you should do more listening than talking, and where your will dies and you submit to God's will for your life. It's during your devotional time that you let God know what's on your mind, what you are dealing with, and what you need Him to do in your life.

Conversely, it's a time to let God deal with you about the things He wants to address in your life, such as His purpose for your life or what He created you to uniquely do; the goals you should be working toward in each and every area of your life; those people He wants you to reach out to and help; the books He's placed in you to write and help others; and perhaps that missions trip He needs you to go on. And if you let Him deal with you about these things, He helps you with what you are concerned about as well.

Our devotional life is also a time to worship and praise the Lord when no one else is around, to express to Him how much we love and need Him in our lives. It's in that context where we can grasp a deeper revelation of who He really is. It's also a time not just to read but to dig in and study His Word, asking God to open it up to us so we understand what it means, what it looks like when we walk in it, and how to apply it in our lives.

While we should spend time throughout the day communicating with God, our devotional life should be how we start our day, in the same place and at the same time each day to the extent possible—just like Miss Clara did in the movie *War Room*. Where is your war room? God gave us His best when He gave His Son's life so we could have life again in Him, so we should give Him our best as we start each day. Starting our day with a devotional time also prepares us for the challenges, trials, tribulations, and opportunities we will face as we go about our day in a lost and dying world.

If you don't have a devotional life, MoC, start one right where you are. If you already have a devotional life, let God evaluate it and show you how you can go deeper in your personal relationship with Him. That's what your devotional life should really be all about, continually developing and going deeper in your personal relationship with God so that as you go about your daily life, you are an expression of the Lord for all of the world to see—Him living through you.

If you want some help on how to develop a consistent devotional life, go to the News page on my website (faithprinciples.net), and scroll down to the interview I did several years ago with my pastor, Bishop Jeffery A. Williams, titled "Build It Like This! Morning Decree," in which I detail the nine aspects of my own devotional life which helps me to continue growing each day and walking as a MoC.

You might be asking why I didn't just include the details of my devotional life in this book. I could have, but referring you to my website requires you to take some action beyond just reading this book. It causes you to make an effort to learn something that might help you in your own walk through an additional investment of your time. As I have learned over my lifetime, you only get out of something what are willing to put into it. If you're reading this book, you've already made one investment of your time, energy, and mind to grow as a MoC. Why not make another and see if there's anything I do as part of my devotional life that might help you with yours?

Chapter Eleven

PRINCIPLE #9
STAND IN
THE GAP

The ninth principle of biblical manhood is that *the MoC stands in the gap for his brothers and sisters.* Ezekiel 22:30 states, "So I sought for a man among them who would make a wall, and stand in the gap before Me on behalf of the land, that I should not destroy it; but I found no one." This informs us that God is looking for men to stand in the gap between Him and the land so He won't destroy it because of its wickedness. But what does this mean exactly?

Simply stated, to stand in the gap for someone or something is to stand up for, defend, and speak and/or act on behalf of someone or something. As it relates to this principle, it means to stand up for, defend, and speak and/or act on behalf of your family, loved ones, friends, and brothers and sisters in Christ.

You do this by intervening and interceding for them before God, praying for them, asking God to have mercy upon them and to bestow His grace on them. Furthermore, you commit to help them in their Christian walk, standing with them if the need arises as they repent and turn back to God. You support and encourage them, cover them, and/or have their back as it were. All this is what we see that many of the Old Testament prophets did, and our Lord Jesus did the same when He prayed for all mankind (see John 17:6-26).

You might want to do as I do and think about who is depending upon you and who needs your help and prayers to keep in your mind who needs you to stand in the gap for them. For example, I pray for the wellbeing, strength, covering, protection, support, wisdom, direction, and guidance of my pastor and his family every day, and specifically for challenges he has shared with me at times with which he is dealing in his life.

There are certain brothers in Christ struggling right now with certain issues who I pray for. I call them on a regular basis to support and ask how I can help. I may provide a ride to an event, treat to a meal, or sometimes just hang out with them if they need someone to talk to. During our discussions, sometimes I provide correction (which as MoCs, we need to be humble enough to seek out and receive when we know we need it). There are yet others who I've loaned money to meet an immediate need. Then, spend time with them, sharing my knowledge of finance and budgeting to empower them to be better stewards of the money God has blessed them with now, so they can prepare for the harvest God has in store for them as they demonstrate more effective financial stewardship.

As a MoC, we should always be standing in the gap on behalf of and praying for our wives, children, unsaved loved ones, and those we know of and care about who may be afflicted with sickness, illness, and disease. There's one brother I know who was suffering from severe spinal issues and nerve damage who I called on regularly to try and encourage him by sharing the testimony of my own struggles with arthritis and how my faith in God as well as praying for the healing of others helped me to receive my healing. He asked me to come to his house and lay hands on him and anoint him with oil as an ordained elder of the Church according to James 5:14-15:

> Is anyone among you sick? Then he must call for the elders of the church and they are to pray over him, anointing him with oil in the name of the Lord; and the prayer of faith will restore the one who is sick, and the Lord will raise him up, and if he has committed sins, they will be forgiven him.

I didn't "feel" like going over to his house on that Saturday morning as I had other things I needed to do, but it was more important as a MoC to stand in the gap for my brother. So I went to his house, prayed for him, laid hands on him, and anointed him with oil, and immediately he started moving much better and his pain started to subside.

In Luke 10:25-37, we have the story of the Good Samaritan. Recently a brother in Christ shared a message from this passage on Sunday morning and taught that this is really a lesson about four types of people. First, there were the priest and the Levite who saw the man on the side of the road who had been beaten by robbers. They crossed over to the other side of the road to avoid the beaten man, one not wanting to get involved and the other thinking it was below him to reach out and help.

Then there was the innkeeper who was only interested in taking advantage of the beaten man's condition for his own gain to get as much money out of the situation as he could. Only the Samaritan man, not even a Jew, had compassion for the beaten man and stood in the gap for him in his helpless condition, nursing his wounds and taking him to a place where he could rest, be cared for, and be restored to health—all at the Samaritan's expense.

So I ask you, MoC, do you stand in the gap for your wife, children, family members, church, pastor, and brothers and sisters in Christ? Do you want them to stand in the gap for you when need be (and we all need others standing in the gap for us from time to time)? Then stand in the gap for them! You do this not only or even primarily so they will stand in the gap for you, but rather to be able to answer God's call for the MoC to stand in the gap so you will be able to say, "Here I am, Lord."

Chapter Twelve

PRINCIPLE #10

HONOR YOUR TEMPLE

The 10th principle of biblical manhood is that *the MoC honors his temple.* "I beseech you therefore, brethren, by the mercies of God, that you present your bodies a living sacrifice, holy, acceptable to God, which is your reasonable service" (Romans 12:1). Paul wrote those words to instruct us that we should present our bodies as living sacrifices to God in an acceptable manner.

Think about all God did for you, even dying for you through His only Son Jesus so you could be reconciled to Him. This then allowed you to inherit eternal life as well as all the other benefits of salvation like healing and health, deliverance and restoration, peace and prosperity. When you consider that, the least you should want to do is keep your body, which is the temple God lives in through His Holy Spirit, in the best shape you can so it's a vessel worthy for Him to live in, physically, spiritually, morally, emotionally—and in every other way.

Paul wrote in 1 Corinthians 6:18-20,

> Flee sexual immorality. Every sin that a man does is outside the body, but he who commits sexual immorality sins against his own body. Or do you not know that your body is the temple of the Holy Spirit who is in you, whom you have from God, and you are not your own? For you were bought at a price; therefore glorify God in your body and in your spirit, which are God's.

Paul was clear that we should shun the practice of sexual immorality, a sin against our own body, which is the temple through which God lives in us and now belongs to God and no longer to ourselves. Therefore, we can't do whatever we want with our bodies like we once did. This Scripture also tells us that we should glorify God with our bodies.

Let's look at another passage on this topic: "That each of you should know how to possess his own vessel in sanctification and honor, not in passion of lust, like the Gentiles who do not know God" (1 Thessalonians 4:4-5). From this we learn that we should control or take care of our bodies, setting them aside for service unto God, honoring them as the temples through which God lives in us.

Now these passages are often understood to be about physical fitness, and they do pertain to that, but they are not limited to just that. They also speak to keeping our bodily temple fit spiritually as well as physically. Some people, for example, are infatuated with staying physically fit while paying little or no attention to keeping the body spiritually fit. God is telling us to do both since our bodies no longer belong to us but to God through Christ. We're now stewards over our bodies with an obligation to keep them worthy for God to reside in through the Holy Spirit so He can rely on them to do the work of the Kingdom.

We do this by eating right, exercising, getting enough sleep, and not abusing our bodies with things such as sexual immorality, alcohol, tobacco, drugs, lack of exercise, etc. For example, not abusing ourselves with sexual immorality includes refraining from lust, pornography, fornication/adultery, same sex relations, masturbation, etc. Eating right and getting proper exercise require doing your homework, consulting with your physician to set proper weight goals for your height, body shape, and age, having an effective diet plan, and establishing the right exercise routine or regimen for your body.

Not doing things to abuse your body also means not going to some of the places you used to go to, not hanging out with some of the people you used to hang out with, being mindful of what you watch and listen to through the media so as not to temp yourself unnecessarily with things that could lead you to abusing your body. It further means getting help, because most of us aren't strong enough to do these things on our own. And the help I'm talking about is both accountability partners from among people you know who will tell you what you need to hear and not what you want to hear, and also in some cases professional help, such as physical trainers, nutritionists, and counselors.

And when you do stumble and fall in any of these areas—which most have and may still do from time to time—you must confess your sins, accept God's forgiveness, and repent, which may again include getting help from others in the form of counseling. Above all, don't beat yourself up or think God won't forgive you or that you'll never be able to get your temple/body in order. That's exactly what the devil wants you to think. Rather, turn back to God and agree with Him that you sinned and walk in the forgiveness that is already yours through Jesus! Furthermore, let repentance have its full impact on you. Repentance is not an event but a process. It takes time to study the Word until you truly change your thinking so you can then change your walk, get your temple in order, and maintain it. I was able to do that, and if God did that for me, He'll surely do it for you too!

When we treat our bodies as the temples they are, we not only please God, but we are also able to be used by Him to go where He wants us to go, say what He wants us to say, and do what He wants us to do, all for the furthering of His Kingdom on the earth. None of this would be possible if our bodies are broken down, sick, or defiled and ravaged by sin. In addition, we then feel good about ourselves and can live the abundant life God wants us to have. The same applies to keeping ourselves fit spiritually, morally, and emotionally.

So we need to examine ourselves, MoC, and let God show each of us, if we don't already know, what areas we have *not* been honoring and being good stewards over our bodily temples. When He shows you, then repent and submit to God's will in that area, and commit to do something about it. Be a MoC who honors his temple in every area. Whatever it is you need to do to honor God with your temple, be about it, MoC, so He can use you and bless you as He wants to.

Chapter Thirteen

PRINCIPLE #11

SAY WHAT YOU MEAN AND MEAN WHAT YOU SAY

Principle #11 of biblical manhood is that *the MoC says what he means and means what he says.* This principle goes back to the "I" of the CIA of being a MoC of integrity. Yes, integrity means being honest and open, and per the dictionary means firm adherence to a code of moral values. As integrity relates to this CIA principle of manhood, it focuses mostly on being a man of your word. As one of my former pastors who is now with the Lord used to teach the men in the church I attended, a man is only as good as his word. Your word should be your bond, something that can be relied upon without question, something that those dependent on what you say can count on you to do.

How many times, however, do people, including most if not all in the church as well, say they will do something but then don't? They say

"Yes, I'll attend this meeting or that event," and then don't. "You can count on me to do this or that," and then don't. "I've got your back on that," but then don't. It would have been better if they hadn't committed to do anything at all, or at least let someone know they weren't going to be able to follow through on what they committed to do.

But the MoC honors his word at almost any cost, saying what he means and meaning what he says. I say at *almost* any cost because there may be extenuating circumstances that arise from time to time that prevent him from doing what he says, such as family or work emergencies. But when that happens, the MoC lets the person(s) he has committed to help know he can't keep his commitment as far in advance as possible rather than at the last minute or not at all. He also does all he can to get someone else to fulfill the commitment he has made.

Proverbs 11:3 states, "The integrity of the upright will guide them, but the perversity of the unfaithful will destroy them." Being a person of integrity will guide us in the right way to go but being unfaithful and determined to do the opposite of what is expected will destroy those who do so. We learn from Proverbs 20:7, "The righteous man walks in his integrity; his children are blessed after him," that if we live a life of righteousness and integrity, the blessings it brings will not only come to us but to our children after us.

Another reason a MoC strives to be a man of his word is because it's a sin not to do so! Did you know that? Psalms 76:11a says "Make vows to the Lord your God and fulfill them," and Matthew 5:33 states, "Again, you have heard the ancients were told 'You shall not make false vows, but shall fulfill your vows to the Lord.'" So when we don't honor the vow we make when we give our word to someone, it's the same as not keeping a vow, which we see in these two verses is contrary to God's Word and is therefore clearly sinful behavior!

Not only that, but when we don't keep our word or vow, it's actually lying, which we know from Proverbs 6:16-17 God detests: "There are six things God hates, Seven that are an abomination to Him: Haughty eyes, a lying tongue ..." You must remember that when you state openly to one or more people something you intend to do, it impacts more than just yourself. Other people are counting and depending on you to do what you said, sometimes making plans or commitments of their own to do something based on your word about what you are going to do. So when you don't keep your word, there's a ripple effect that negatively impacts others who were counting on you to keep your word. Not only that, but your reputation, the trust people have in you, is negatively impacted. Other people's opinion of your reliability and trustworthiness diminishes, and once it does, it can take a lot of time and effort on your part to build it back up again.

Why is it that people don't keep or ignore commitments they've made as often as they do? Distractions and being governed by one's feelings are the primary reasons. They begin to talk themselves out of their commitment, convincing themselves they don't have time or need the rest. But this is not how the MoC should be.

One example from my own life goes back almost 30 years ago when I was a district manager over an engineering and construction operation across an entire state for a large telecommunications company. In those days when we expanded the availability of landline telephone facilities, it sometimes resulted in the laying of significant new telephone line routes, both aerial and underground, all terminating at a central location where the new facilities were assigned to customers and maintained called a Central Office or CO. When the work was done and everything was tested, ready to go, and the time came to put the new facilities into service, it was usually done with a big celebratory event with the "cut over" of the new facilities going into service at midnight on a Friday night with many company and local civic officials being invited.

In one such case where my engineering and construction teams had been quite involved in the work, I was invited to the midnight cut over which was in a different state and about 45 minutes away. Because I said I would attend, some special arrangements were made to acknowledge the work my team and I had contributed to the project.

However, I didn't show up. I had intended to, but made every excuse I could to myself as to why it was unreasonable for me to go, things like, "I'm too tired; I don't really need to be there; it's been a hard week and I don't really want to go all the way back for this; they won't miss me." I found out that it did matter. This was a big deal to a lot of people, and me coming meant a lot, especially being the highest ranking minority manager for the company in that state at the time.

I let a lot of people down, hurt my credibility as a person of integrity, and got sidetracked as a result in my career advancement for a period of time. Fortunately, I was able to come back from that setback and still do well in my career with that company, but it took me a little longer to do so than it could have. I didn't advance as far as I could have because I had a "weak moment" and was not a man of my word—saying what I mean and meaning what I say.

Now let's consider an example in the Bible. Joseph, the stepfather of Jesus and husband of Mary, is a good biblical example of a man of integrity. Joseph was betrothed to Mary, which was a public statement that he intended to marry her and keep her as his wife. When Joseph learned of Mary's pregnancy before their marriage had been consummated, he probably could not fathom her story of how this occurred and had some options to consider. He could have brought her before the religious leaders for her to be punished according to the Law; he could divorce her quietly and separate himself from Mary without completely humiliating both of them; or he could have married her anyway and be known as the fool who married an adulteress.

Originally he decided to try and spare both their reputations as best as he could by divorcing her quietly, but then an angel appeared to him in a dream to confirm Mary's account of how she became pregnant, instructing him to proceed with the marriage. Being a good man, he did just that and followed through on what he said he would do despite realizing that many would not believe how Mary became pregnant.

The lesson from theses examples is that we need to strive to be men of our word all of the time, not just when we feel like it, or when it's convenient to do, or when it only puts us in good standing before men. Therefore, let's take inventory of how we stack up as men of integrity. asking ourselves, "How good is my word? Can I be counted on to follow through on what I say I will do? What do I do when I can't keep a commitment I have made?" These and others are questions for you to mull over and answer privately for yourself and before God. But the bottom line, men, is to make sure we say what we mean and mean what we say.

Chapter Fourteen

PRINCIPLE #12

MODEL YOUR LIFE AFTER CHRIST

The last principle of biblical manhood I want to share is that the *MoC models his life after Jesus.* Our Savior, Lord, Master, and Ruler showed us how to live as godly men when He walked on the earth as a man. Although He was God, He came down to our level and became flesh just like us, subject to all of the temptations, trials, tribulations, and attacks from the enemy that we are as described in Philippians 2:5-8:

> Let this mind be in you which was also in Christ Jesus, who, being in the form of God, did not consider it robbery to be equal with God, but made Himself of no reputation, taking the form of a bond-servant, and coming in the likeness of men. And being found in appearance as a man, He humbled Himself and became obedient to the point of death, even the death of the cross.

He overcame death through complete submission to God, which means He willingly came under God's authority and was obedient to God's Word. And He did this as a man, just like we are. So if He did it and He is our role model, then we can do it too! Modeling our lives after Jesus starts with complete submission to God.

There are so many other traits involved in modeling our lives after Jesus that I could not possibly cover them all in this book. So I encourage you to read the gospels of Matthew, Mark, Luke, and John and study the character of Jesus. Examine how He lived His life and compare that to how you're living your life. As you do, identify areas where you need to be more like Jesus, then repent for not having done so, and change your mind to a Kingdom way of thinking. This takes work and effort on your part to find out how Jesus lived, what He did in challenging situations similar to those you face, and then work on them, one area or trait at a time.

However, there are four traits of Jesus' lifestyle or character in addition to submission that I read in a newsletter from the Christian Roundtable Group several years ago I want to leave with you. These four have stuck with me, and are traits which I believe all MoCs (and women) should strive to emulate:

> 1) *Jesus resisted passivity*. Jesus was not unresponsive to actions taken against Him. He always responded, and His response was always based on the Word of God. So don't sit back and let things happen or let nature take its course, as we like to say. We have a responsibility to respond to the issues of life and not

let them keep us in bondage. However, we should do so based on directives from the Word of God just like Jesus did and not actions based on circumstances, feelings, and emotions.

2) *Jesus was courageous.* He didn't back down from whatever was before Him but took it on with boldness and confidence, knowing it was the will of God. The Bible tells us that God has given us not a spirit of fear but of power and of a sound mind (see 2 Timothy 1:7). Therefore, don't run from the issues of life, but be a man like Jesus was and face up to whatever is before you—in other words, be a MoC.

3) *Jesus was responsible.* He was accountable and fulfilled the purpose God had assigned for Him on earth, which was to seek and save the lost by dying for the sins of all mankind. What's God's purpose for or call on your life? Are you living it out or making up excuses as to why you can't fulfill it right now? Maybe the first question to ask is, "Do you know God's purpose for your life?" If not, ask Him, seek His wisdom on the matter, and He will tell you. But if you already know God's will for your life, then as the MoC, you need to be about living it out.

4) *Jesus looked to the greater eternal rewards of heaven.* Jesus knew He would go back to the Father who would be well pleased with Him for what He had done on earth. He looked forward to

the joy He would have in what He did for you, me, and all of mankind. What's your reward or joy you're looking forward to by carrying out God's will for your life? Stayed focused on that and let it be a motivator to keep you moving in God's will for your life. Who is it that's depending on you or who needs what carrying out God's Will for your life will bring to them?

You are the answer to somebody's prayer. You are their miracle waiting to happen. Stay focused on the joy it will give you to be a blessing to others and please the Father, and let that keep you going, motivated to live out God's purpose for your life. So keep your eyes on Jesus, MoC, and strive to model your life after that of the King.

Chapter Fifteen

WHAT NOW?

You might be thinking to yourself, "Wow, this is a lot. Where do I go from here? How do I go about establishing and applying these pillars and principles of biblical manhood in my life to enhance my walk as a MoC?" The short answer is one step or truth at a time. What does that mean? Glad you asked, so let me explain.

The first thing you need to do is to review a short, concise summary of what I've shared with you in this book to get your mind and heart around the gist of being a MoC in as few words as possible. In an attempt to bring together all of what the Lord has shared through me in this book, here is a brief summary you can use of what it means to be a MoC. Feel free to customize it in any way that better fits your needs.

- Being a male is a matter of birth, while being a man is a matter of choice.

- A covenant relationship is an agreement between two or more parties that cannot be broken without penalty, injury or death, But Jesus has already paid the price for any brokenness in our covenant relationship with God. It's up to us, however, to choose to claim and walk in what Jesus has done for us.

- The three pillars or building blocks of biblical manhood or being a MoC are Commitment (bound to or tied to the Word of God), Integrity (living out what you say you believe in private as well as in public) and Accountability (taking responsibility for your actions and the actions of those under your authority), the (CIA) of biblical manhood.

A MoC lives out these pillars in his life through application of the following principles:

1. Is a learned disciple of the Lord Jesus Christ, and a student of the Word of God.

2. Lives by the Word of God as the final authority and absolute rule of conduct for his life.

3. Strives to live righteously, not deliberately or intentionally disobeying the Word of God, which is referred to as sinning.

4. Repents when he sins.

5. Puts the needs of his family and others above his own.

6. Honors and respects his parents, loves his wife like Jesus does the Church, and raises his children according to the Word of God.

7. Walks by faith and not by sight.

8. Has a devotional life and prays daily.

9. Stands in the gap for his brothers and sisters.

10. Honors his bodily temple.

11. Says what he means and means what he says.

12. Models his life after Jesus.

If you need to review any of the principles, you can go back and reread the chapter which discusses it in greater detail. Most importantly, as you review the three pillars and twelve principles of being a MoC, ask God for wisdom and revelation as to what's behind the words—what they mean, what His intent is for a MoC to walk in them? Remember, during this review stage, the goal is not to figure out how to apply them in your life, but to gain a deeper understanding of what they will look like when you apply them in your life.

Now that you've finished this initial review, you're ready to start the process of applying them in your life or enhancing the depth and quality of your walk in them if you're already applying all or some of them. Here's how I go about doing that, but by all means develop the process that works best for you.

1. Go over the list of principles and ask God to reveal which ones you're applying in your life now and which ones you're not.

2. Assess how effectively you're walking in those you are already applying based on how you see yourself doing, all the while seeking God's wisdom as to how you are doing, perhaps asking some other MoC who are already walking in many of these principles about what they do or what they think of your walk.

3. Develop a priority list of the principles

you need to work on and in which order, based on

a) whether or not you're walking in a particular principle right now;

b) how well you're walking in the principles you are already applying in your life based on number two above; and

c) the importance of each principle in your life, which requires that you again need to seek God's wisdom and perhaps ask other MoCs who are already walking in many of these principles to share their perspective.

4. Develop a plan based on numbers one through three above for applying or improving a specific principle in your life, one principle at a time based upon the priority you establish.

5. Work or implement the plan you've developed.

6. Periodically assess how you're doing based on your own perception, input from other MoCs, and, most importantly, input from God.

7. Revise your plan based on your assessment in number six above, and start working on a revised plan.

By way of example, when I first did this review in my own life, it became clear to me that there were several of these principles I needed to focus on more than the others: standing in the gap for my brothers and sisters, honoring my body or temple, and (fully) repenting when I sin—in that order.

Beginning with the highest priority principle that I had to work on first, I did a more in-depth study in the Word about what this principle meant in general, but more specifically for me, as discussed in Principle 9 in this book. I was open to whatever God showed me as to the changes I needed to make to truly apply or walk out this principle in my life. I looked for both biblical examples of MoCs in the Bible walking out this principle, as well as MoCs who exemplified it today.

I then studied what they did to see how I might walk this out in my life, including talking with peer MoCs who exemplified this principle and had wisdom that I could access. What I found was that I wasn't really putting the needs of others above my own or having the best interests of others at heart to the extent I thought I did. I may have said I did, but my actions did not support what I said. I didn't want to inconvenience myself and wasn't as flexible or willing to sacrifice something I wanted to do for the sake of helping someone else. If this sounds familiar or maybe even like you, I think you and I have a lot of company in the body of Christ who are the same way.

That takes us to the next step, which was to develop and implement a plan for improving my application of this principle in my life with God's guidance and direction, using feedback from God, myself, and other MoCs. For me, this meant being purposeful and intentional about being more alert to the needs of others than I had been, and then doing whatever I could to express God's love to them by showing compassion and helping them as opportunities presented themselves.

For example, instead of just saying hello and

asking how others were doing after Sunday service, especially with people I didn't know that well, I started to take the time to ask about their family, their career, how things were going at home, in their marriage, with their children at work, with their walk with God. I was surprised at how many people were hurting, even in the body of Christ, to whom an extended conversation meant a lot.

But I had to go beyond just the extended conversation when they shared with me issues they were facing in their lives. I had to try and help in the best way I could. This in itself sometimes required seeking God's wisdom, but often it meant setting a time to get together with them over coffee or a meal to talk about their issue in more depth and help them work towards a solution. Sometimes it meant hooking them up with someone more qualified than I who could help them or finding someone or some resources that could help them. Sometimes it involved blessing them financially. Other times it was just a smile, handshake, hug, or listening to them that was needed.

The other thing I had to do was to intentionally and purposefully follow-up with people to see how they were progressing and how things were going or had turned out, asking if there was anything else I could do for them or anything I could pray with them about. All this was about developing a "relationship" with the people I was standing in the gap for.

This is an iterative process which you keep revisiting as often as necessary. Once I got better at standing in the gap for people, I had to and still have to be intentional about standing in the gap for people, but I could now move on to the next MoC principle on my priority list on which I needed to work.

Another thing that's a good idea to do is to periodically, at least annually, go back to step one and reassess where you are in your MoC walk, reevaluating what your priorities are. We all change, develop, and grow over time, and as we do the priorities of what we need to focus on in any given area of our lives change—as do the seasons. If it seems like this process never ends, you are correct! But the more you work at it, the more walking as a MoC becomes part of your lifestyle.

I pray you have been blessed by this impartation the Lord gave me to share with you, and I challenge you to make the choice to live as a man of covenant. Be who God created you to be and already sees you to be—as He chose you to be before the beginning of time (see Ephesians 1:4-6). Don't let this be just another book you've read which then sits on your bookshelf collecting dust. Use it as a resource and guide throughout your walk with the Lord and become who He called you to be!

In His name!

ABOUT THE AUTHOR

RUSSELL B. GROSS JR

Russell is a native Rhode Islander with an engineering degree from the state university. Russ had successful business careers in telecommunications and healthcare, and was quite active in promoting diversity in the workplace and community. He gave his life to the Lord over 40 years ago and since then has freely given of his time, talent, and treasure to serve the Kingdom of God. He has led the men's and prison ministries and chaired the board of directors at his local church, The King's Cathedral, in Providence, R.I. Russ has authored five books on financial stewardship, faith, succeeding in the workplace and living as a man of covenant, and has taught biblically-based courses on these topics and others at his local church and in the community.

Since retiring from the corporate world in late 2016, he has continued to "take care of Kingdom business" through writing and conducting workshops for community-based organizations to empower people so they can know the Lord, express His purpose, and experience prosperity in every area of their lives—at home, at work, at church, and in the community. Russ currently resides in Mansfield, Massachusetts with his wife, Roberta, and they are the parents of two adult sons and three granddaughters. He also enjoys playing golf, listening to music, and traveling.

Contact Russell Gross

Website: wwwfaithprinciples.net

Email – elderrussfaithprinciples@gmail.com

His books are available on Amazon and
www.faithprinciples.net

Kingdom Prosperity: God's Plan for Successful Financial Stewardship

Faith: The Currency of the Kingdom

The Power of PIE: How A Man of Color and a Follower of Christ Succeeded in Corporate America

More Than Faith

Man Of Covenant